The Saying of Names

Karen Blaylock
The Saying of Names

Acknowledgements

Poems in this collection have appeared in the *Adelaide Review*, *Canberra Times*, *Quadrant*, *Heat*, *Poetrix*, *Vernacular*, *Friendly Street Readers*, *Studio*, *The Quadrant Book of Poetry 2012* (ed. Les Murray) and the Hills Poets anthology *Ripples*. Several of the poems have been read on Radio 5UV.

The Saying of Names
ISBN 978 1 76109 331 9
Copyright © Karen Blaylock 2022

First published 2022 by
Ginninderra Press
PO Box 3461 Port Adelaide 5015
www.ginninderrapress.com.au

Contents

In the Garden	7
Spinning Top	8
Bridge Lingering	9
Hot Day	10
Everyday Watch	11
Dusk	12
Fisherman's Life, Fisherman's Wife	13
Sonnet	14
Night Shiver	15
Four Short Poems	16
Rejected Poems	17
Boy With a Paddle	18
Refrain	19
The Saying of Names	20
Bird in Late Spring	21
Giving the Nod to Rain	22
October Rains	23
Magnolia and Leaves	24
Sparrow Song	25
Mother's Day	26
Po Chu-I	27
Shrinking	28
After Horace	29
What's What and Which is Which	30
Light	31
Bird Calls in July	32
Spring Light and Rains	33
Courtyard	34
Ode to the Way	35
Come Any Time	36

Dreamers	37
Seals	38
Beautiful in Black	39
Vignette	40
Mystery	41
The Poetry of Leisure	42
No Poor Indifferent Place	43

In the Garden

(In loving memory of Papa)

In the garden, I followed you around,
nothing happened, nothing and
everything that is, time was gold,
chat was made of neither this nor that.
Little unsaid fluencies flowered
between us, we shared an affinity
for green and rain, and when the coloured
summer came, we were an audience of two.

I see us now in that suburban yard,
the light has crystallised, afternoon
shadows come in like the cat to her milk,
the sprinkler makes roses of water in
the reddening sun, we sit looking on,
as if there were nothing else in the world,
but you and I, and the garden.

Spinning Top

There were times, on a wet day,
I had the run of the lino floor,
For a go with the top, to send it away:
There was wishing in the pump, for
                          absolute or more.
The silver-twisted stem disappeared, hazed;
All-the-time twirling. Shapes amassed,
Bright tin colours blurred: then the thrall.

Perfection sailed around the room. In the spin
my centre was true, hover and tensile held:
I loved to see the animals come home, return
To form; reds, greens and others, differ from
                                the meld.
As the spin slurred to watchable, and petered out,
I came back, from some far-flung haunt.

Bridge Lingering

You slow the boat and drift beneath the bridge
Where the river's lost its light,
The acoustic is all grey-stone-edge,
The water dense; a drabness to it.
Lingering around the city's danker
Side eying damp graffiti, stilled by the
Under-arch arrangement, sunless water
And circular stone – one pacifies the other.

As our hoots reverberated round the vault
I listened to the echoes mix and fade,
Like sounds from the underworld
Eerie yet cathedral light
Then coming out of shadow, into green
Clarity and light, and the world reborn.

Hot Day

The shrill midsummer sun
a steely-voiced soprano
silvering sky
lasering grass
oiling cowhides
on hillsides

The air,
spaces between green,
burns white hot
like a dissolving
magnesium flare

Tender leaves
frizzle,
crisper than autumn

Native plants
rise to the heat,
grinning.

Everyday Watch

It's not the gold I inherited from you, but
The everyday platinum, forgotten
In a drawer, honest face, a hundred years extant,
Keeping time like a conscientious railwayman.

Sentiment doesn't fit with it, but in the
Steel smooth from wear and in all seventeen
Jewels, there's you; diamonds of silver
As numbers, the tick like the rhythm of a train.

Dusk

We missed the astonishing light and came
Home with burning ridges and sky-pastels
That were as compliments on our sane
Southern hills: light distils and distils.
Animals leave their shady haunts, they seem to grieve,
Trees reveal an emphasis of form
Against a dusk that if you look, is made of
More events, than anyone would dream.

Fisherman's Life, Fisherman's Wife

Fishing sounded good, so clean I thought,
Simple and sanctioned, an air about it;
Those souls who cast their nets at first light,
In plain boats, weren't they the very salt.

It was diesel, grease, pubs and yarns, it was
Dragging the ocean floor; the odd Flat
Caught among the shells – a silver prize
Delivered, with the smile, of a cat.

We watched you leave the wharf, the child and I,
All three of us in moonlight, the sea singing
With it, you did the ropes like fisherman's t'ai
chi, and were gone like an eel swimming.

Sonnet

All this backward drift to then
When now is more properly in-place
Earthed, like the second half, for Jung
Like an increase of rain, a greenness.
I liked, at school, in history
The feudal way with fields
A rich and deep security
A working beat, as elder time yields.

Could it be as Eliot grandly said
The past not finished, the future not before us
By which I, not properly schooled, read
All cuts of time have relevance.
It was snail-like in coming, the honouring
Of every pure and brackish thing.

Night Shiver

(In July)

Clouds move across in china-painting pink
Sheep have gathered from their wandering,
Something sad in cows with the light sinking,
They look like the homeless heading home.

Everything is slow in this closing of shades
Except for birds who come in low, trapezers
In the stillness. The garden blackens as
The sky goes through its curious blues.

Looking through the window at the last
Light, there's a point before the stars are
Out, or even blackness, that's as cold as glass,
When you shut out the night with a shiver.

Four Short Poems

One hundred thoughts –
a shower of blossom
blows them free.

The first rain
like an upside-down
prayer.

Sheep run downhill
as if it mattered.

Happiness is American
contentment is biblical.

Rejected Poems

Rejected poems come home
like poor relations
of themselves

Boy With a Paddle

It was early morning on the river of green glass
in soft sunlight and the stillness and near-silence
of the water and once in a while an ibis
sensing our coming flying white in daylight as
on we went until it happened in a moment,
the snake swimming ahead of the prow of
the canoe, all our astonishment and the beauty of it
stilled in time you can't assess, our paths
foreseeably crossing glide on glide, it reared then
a fiery S up and half inside the boat and
the boy on his wits struck and we watched the fencing
and the dance, till the snake all done slipped
into the water and was gone and we went our way
on the mirror of the river in the morning.

Refrain

I'm behind the times, painting light and air,
geraniums, wrens, cockatoos, galahs,
trees and green and rain, as if they were love,
as if to please the earth with songs;

the way religious take a vow,
keeping faith, the way I'm doing now,
starting afresh with the same all over again,
like Monet, down by the lilies, with his canvas in the sun.

The Saying of Names

Morning sunlight on the paper
of the page that I am reading
and in the glimmer
of the moment of being
it's silk-like, this paper in the light,
the white weave has shimmers
of grey and the sheen is like skin
and the poet I am reading,
the way I read sun and shadow
on the texture of the page,
has only memories and light,
all has vanished it seems
and yet goes on, nameless and silent
but wait, words turn
as the world is turning
while here in the garden
it is winter again,
a story as old as the telling
as old as the saying of names.

Bird in Late Spring

The wattle droops after rain
pods coming on blue for Christmas
bees drone to the point of noise
in a tree grown for shade and
me, I'm in the garden taking
in the colours of nasturtiums
and roses scattered after rain
and now there's a pigeon
flying in low, the sound of its wings
softening the silence, grey body in
a grey white light, in branches now
and thickened leaves and just as soon
flying upward into clouds of felt
and it happened in moments
with the garden green and calm and
home to the spirit of the bird, just then.

Giving the Nod to Rain

I remember just these skies at just this time
of year, gardening in and out of rain,
how you called the weather show'ry,
pronouncing it with care, never wishing
things to be other than they were.
It was patience filled the intervals,
enough for you and me. The clearings came
like miracles of light, and if it turned
to weather, we'd shelter and listen
to the dance on tin and you'd deliver
your amen, 'gives em a good drink'
was all you said and made it sound
like something; you'd give a nod
and rock heel-toe, and say the same again.

October Rains

Light October rains falling across the hills
and garden and half the spring flowers
raining, heavens what a sight, paths of bells
and petals, of one sort or another,
layer on layer on the black earth and
even the street. Snow fell out of the ordinary once
and it was and wasn't like this; the sounds
outside are quiet, bird calls few and I'm
alone here in the house and the rain
slantwise from the window, friends have gone
to ground so I take to reading poems,
lives that are and are not like mine
and the words so long ago in time
not so distant, through the light and rain.

Magnolia and Leaves

(After a painting)

Quite clever to paint love, confessional like this,
to leave your heart in the workings of a flower,
petals, crème de la crème, olivine leaves.

I muse on metamorphosis,
the secret of stillness, the secret of the dance,
and something of the scent, of bliss.

You wouldn't think you could fall for leaves
but I have, green leaves in a curved vase;
magnolia flower as sensuous as love.

Sparrow Song

All the world at perfect pitch
the stars aligned in spring
all the world a lowly hum
as the blackbirds sing
and sparrows at the waterbath

All the early trees in leaf
and flowers by the door
apple-blossoms all-at-once
butterflies galore
and sparrows at the waterbath

Pigeons fly across the yard
away, away in pairs
at four o'clock the light is blessed
all the world at prayers
and sparrows at the waterbath
and sparrows at the waterbath.

Mother's Day

The journey north
through city traffic
the second Sunday
in May

I bring flowers
we chat
admire the cat, why not
autumn at the window
sunlight on the glass

A cup of China tea
then what about a tune
you play with flair
at ninety
I am ten again

We feed the pigeons
on the lawn
remember characters
long gone
you are laughing
in no time

We take our leave
of the place we have come
our whole lives
coming here
so far

Po Chu-I

What brings me to your gate
time without number
none other
than gardens and moss, late

flowers in bloom
autumn
'mist no mist', the moon

So long ago and far
yet only yesterday I had occasion
to mention
the south window

sparrows in leaves
and rain
those I love long gone
birds in the street on the wires.

Shrinking

I bumped into an old lover, he said you've shrunk,
you were tall and willowy once.
My son came home after years away,
he hugged me, he's six foot two, he said you've shrunk.
My mother is shrinking and she thinks I've shrunk.
My neighbour says her whole life is shrinking.
As we stand at the fence and talk about shrinking
the sun fills a Chinese-lantern-flower
with a lantern glow, I watch the colours
deepening, like watching something grow.
I go inside with the makings of a poem
on my mind; just then my editor calls
and says, that's enough backyard poems now,
I know what he's thinking, I've shrunk.

After Horace

Friends, why pester the oracle
preserve its ingenuity
for those matters of terrible
consequence and severity.
Come, each day's a windfall now
the gods are with us in the garden
though their names are long-forgotten.
Take the hour as it's given
what's the future after all,
leave the heavens to their dreaming
and when in a spin, stay still
if you can, and failing that, sing
if you still remember singing;
make something up while listening
to birds in the green laburnum.

What's What and Which is Which

This is where I take a stand, this garden
this is where I say, geranium, wren,
blackbird, blossom-from-heaven and green.
This is where I praise, as if in church
evensong perhaps, or some Latin prayer,
this is where I sing and say
what's what and which is which;

as someone said before me
earth's the ideal place for love.

Light

Driving into Nairne in that spotlit light
that has you thinking of heaven and cartoons;
there must be a word for it somewhere, this light
in some dictionary, or in a poem perhaps

where the sun breaks through purplish-grey cloud
and all you can do is stare at the world
through autumn leaves and out to new green hills
that glow somewhere between emerald

and something more biblical; in light of
sheep out grazing with chiaroscuro
sunshine on their backs; while the earth
sings, brightly and sombrely, Oh.

Bird Calls in July

Topknot pigeon on the cyclone fence
walking steadily along the bar
grey steel, grey pigeon, grey weathered posts;
there is such quietness in grey.

It is mid-July. Bird calls are clear
the sounds are peaceful and pure
the silences, in themselves, are full,
listening is Zen-like. The air is still.

Spring Light and Rains

The countryside is lit with stained-glass light,
the *Book of Kells*, on our Southern hills;
once-in-a-lifetime storms and record rains
have the paddocks greened and heaven-sent.

I know these roads, Mappinga, Riverview,
I know their names, their elms, wild iris,
wood ducks, flying in pairs,
wildness and rush in the seconds that they pass,
then the stillness, of something
that was worth it; like sudden light, and strange.

Courtyard

An outside fire before the sudden rains
the plum blossom sees another spring
the easy silence of cockatoos' wings;
it's hard to say what simple peace they bring.

I suppose this is what the ancients meant
when they talked about the soul at ease:
as I said, the rain came and that was that;
I'll remember it though, that afternoon,
                              those clouds.

Ode to the Way

Caramel-coloured hills, slow against a sky
of misted blue, with autumn arriving
the way the years arrived, unseen;
but who was counting – hardly –
just following the way of *wen*
a sparrow now and then
sun-warmed light in leaves
cabbage moths dancing
butterfly iris flowering
the wind in black bamboo
a crane, like something truthful in the sky.

Come Any Time

Come any time and bring your love of books.
Book-talk suits this unelaborate garden in the hills.
It suits the iron table and these ailing wicker chairs.
It suits the birds. We'll talk about the masters,
Drink another cup and choose our pick,
Praise the ones that changed the world that was;
It's easy talking books beneath the trees
As six or seven spinebills
Dance in branches and in leaves,
Come any time and bring your love of books.

Dreamers

A wolf-whistling bird in the yard
the crab apple out. Winds of September.
I was always a dreamer. My mother said I was *up in the air*.
I liked to stare at clouds. I saw animals and all sorts.
At school, I gazed out the window at the asphalt and the sky.
Once, on Arbour Day, head-down, dreaming on stones
I slammed into a telegraph pole and ricocheted amongst the stars.
That year, Mrs Grey teased one sweet dreaming soul to tears;
she paints pictures now and lately won a prize.
I watch a fly rubbing his hands together by the glass.
I watch the sun reddening leaves called angels' wings,
the centre is a jewel;
I'm thinking it's a passing miracle
I'm thinking I'll make a poem,
one about dreaming, and the colours of the sun.

Seals

Before us, the Southern Ocean, wild
and hushed, where we stood, high above the sea;
seals playing out by the rocks in the bay,
immaculate in small grey waves and wind.
The path curved around the coast
where miniature plants grew like green rosettes,
The Bluff and Granite Island in the haze;
memories rose, and disappeared, like dreams.

We stopped again for seals, in Horseshoe Bay,
sighting them and losing them, in turn;
the thrill of them out there, had us watching
and murmuring, *there, see there*.
We walked back then, and talked softly of pines,
and pigeons, cresting tips of driftwood trees.

Beautiful in Black

(A Song of Long Ago)

Remember when
all our days were summer
and time was ours for keeps

Remember
the serpentine river
sleepy willows and walks

Lovers in a flowered city
the future just a story
our innocence as pretty
as the night was starry

It was winter, the oaks were bare
when the daydream turned to stone
how cold it was that year
waiting for the sap to rise again

I saw you in the city with a lover arm in arm
that smile like Christmas lights
I was travelling south, heading home
to everything I loved, and it was late

Strange to see you standing here alone
the years have disappeared behind our back
In the graveyard, in the rain
you are beautiful in black

Vignette

Cockies sail on sunlit wings
across a swath of green,
flying east against the sun
across the tranquil hills, in June.

Birds in the garden, fly low,
as swift as cockatoos are slow;
I'm looking for a word for peace,
there is only peace.

Mystery

A honeyeater in the lantern flowers,
a blackbird stops on the rail of the fence;
her brown is feather soft,
her outline is complete.

How strange it is, the moment of beauty,
how stillness is eternity
and silence has the clarity of glass
and time, is curiously free.

The Poetry of Leisure

(After the paintings of Leng Mei)

The canvas is the colour of brown paper
making us think of China, long ago,
the folds of her dress flow like a river

his inks are the colours of leaves of sage
lavender stems, shades of brown;
he paints, the poem of the age.

Leng Mei's long gone,
his *Ten Beauties*, gone
the deer beside her, in the garden, gone

yet here he is, Leng Mei,
his hand, his eye,
his courtesans

in the quiet,
in the muted light,
as lovely
as the stillness,
in their way.

No Poor Indifferent Place

(A phrase used by Rilke in *Letters to a Young Poet*)

Was it to say yes, I was in that place
in that very time when on the bank
of the river I listened to reeds
hushing over and over, listened like
some first being to the rushes and
the wind and all the time listening
with those it seemed listening
before, was it for this I made songs.

Was it to say simply it was worth it
to say no poor indifferent place,
the light woven to the rain on the river
circle on circle in the flow,
birds flying at dusk,
the silence that follows,
was it for this I made songs.

www.ingramcontent.com/pod-product-compliance
Lightning Source LLC
Chambersburg PA
CBHW030312100526
44590CB00012B/611